In memory of

Martha Jensen

Placed in the Library of

Sacred Heart School
by Tippe Nine Holers

Sports Stars

NANCY LOPEZ

Wonder Woman of Golf

By Nancy Robison

 CHILDRENS PRESS, CHICAGO

Cover photograph: Richard Pilling
Inside photographs courtesy of the following: Bill Knight Photographer, pages 6, 14, 18, and 31; Richard Pilling, 8; Will Hertzberg, 11, 21, 23, 26, 28, 32, 34, and 40; Sportsphoto photos, 16, 24, and 38.

Library of Congress Cataloging in Publication Data

Robison, Nancy.
  Nancy Lopez: wonder woman of golf.

  (Sports stars)
  SUMMARY: A biography of the young golfer named
the 1978 Ladies Professional Golf Association's Rookie-
of-the-Year and Player-of-the-Year.
    1. Lopez, Nancy—Juvenile literature. 2. Golfers—
United States—Biography—Juvenile literature.
[1. Lopez, Nancy. 2. Golfers. 3. Mexican Americans—
Biography] I. Title. II. Series.
GV964.L67R6   796.352'092'4   [B]   [92]   78-23931
ISBN 0-516-04302-1

    3 4 5 6 7 8 9 10 11 12 R 85 84 83 82 81 80

Sports Stars

NANCY LOPEZ

Wonder Woman of Golf

The most exciting rookie in the history of the Ladies Professional Golf Association (LPGA) is Nancy Lopez. The LPGA began in 1948. Millions of people watch the tournaments on television.

"The first thing I liked about golf was the sound of cleats on cement," says Nancy. "I loved to go to the golf course to hear it."

"When I started playing golf at eight years old, I was a sight," says Nancy. "I was really skinny then. I didn't hit the ball very far, but I hit it straight."

Golf was her first love. Her father, Domingo Lopez, was her first teacher. He too loved the game. When he was not working in his auto shop, he was out playing golf.

Nancy has just putted. She is waiting for the putt to drop.

"When I was nine, Dad entered me in my first tournament," says Nancy. "We played nine holes each day for three days. I was shooting about 62 for nine holes, but I won by 110 strokes."

Nancy was far ahead in the tournament. She even had time to help the others. "Some of the other kids had such a hard time. I teed up the ball for them on the fairway so they could hit it."

Nancy grew up in Roswell, New Mexico. Her parents are Mexican-Americans. In Roswell she won the U.S. Girl's Junior Championship twice. At the age of twelve, Nancy won the New Mexico State Women's Amateur Championship. Before she was in junior high, she won the Roswell city championship.

In the game of golf, the course is marked off into holes. A game may be played in 9, 18, or 36 holes. Each course has a *par*. Par is the number of strokes it should take to get the ball into each hole. A *birdie* is getting the ball in the hole under par by one stroke. A *bogey* is taking an extra stroke over par to get the ball in the hole.

"At first I had a hard time making birdies," Nancy says. "I would choke on short putts. But then Dad started betting me that I wouldn't make them. He kept it up until I started making them. We used to make all kinds of bets. We sometimes bet on who would wash the dishes. But he never let me wash them, even if I lost. He didn't want me to mess up my calluses."

Her putt dropped. Nancy makes a victory sign.

As a young girl, Nancy found it hard to find good golfers. "The older men wouldn't play me because they were afraid they would lose," she says. "The ones I really enjoyed playing with were the guys on the high school team. They'd say, 'Come on, play 36 holes with us.' Once they did that to me four days in a row. The fifth day I was so sick I had to go to the doctor."

As a child, golf lessons were fun for Nancy. But she enjoyed other things too. She took tap-dancing classes, swimming, and gymnastics. She liked to play basketball, volleyball, and touch football.

When she was sixteen, Nancy became the top-ranked amateur golfer in the world. In 1973, she took the golf world by storm. She played in the U.S. Open. She turned down over $4,000 in prize money. She did this to hold on to her amateur standing. Nancy wanted to get more experience. She wanted to play in college before turning pro.

Nancy won the 1976 Western Women's championship. She tied JoAnne Carner for second at the 1975 U.S. Open. Nancy was gaining the title of "Terror of the Tour." She could outdrive her opponent by as much as fifty yards.

"I wasn't mature enough to turn pro after high school," she says. "I couldn't see myself playing college golf for four years, but I wanted to help win the national championships. Besides I had always wanted to go to college."

Making a fairway wood shot.

Nancy won the Association for Intercollegiate Athletics for Women (AIAW) individual title in 1976. Her college team lost the trophy by only one stroke. It was lost to Furman University, in South Carolina, where women's golf is powerful.

"We came so close," Nancy says. "We expected to win, and when we didn't, it was a big letdown."

With Nancy's help, the team did go on to win the title. "There was a lot of pressure on us to win the collegiate title," she says. "You always have pressure from boosters. If you play super one tournament and bad the next, they say, your good play was just luck. You have to keep progressing.

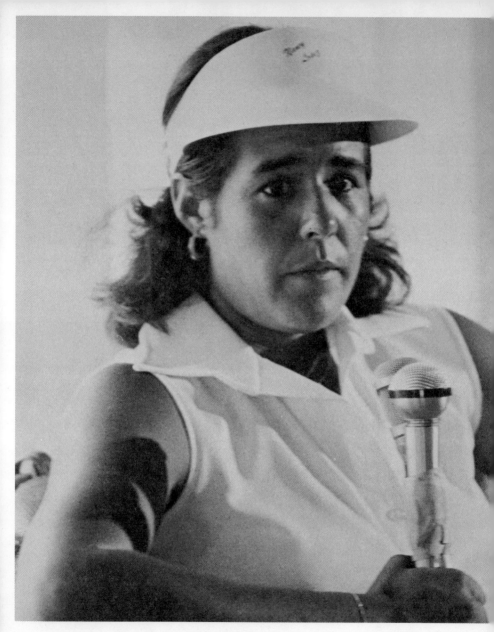

Nancy is interviewed after a tournament.

But you can't play for yourself. Our goal was to be the best team that ever was. We had the talent and we were psyched up. We had everything we needed."

Interested people always have remarks to make to athletes. Nancy has had many well wishes along with other remarks.

"People come up to me on the course and say, 'We're going to win this year, right?' or 'Hitting the ball good, I hope.' or 'Keeping your grades up?' They weren't going to be happy if we lost," Nancy says.

In college, one of Nancy's teammates, Terri Streck, said about her, "When we first heard that

Nancy on the practice tee with her caddie, Roscoe Jones.

Nancy was coming to Tulsa we weren't sure we would like her. Now it seems impossible we ever felt that way. Nancy is genuinely humble. She is such a nice person, you couldn't help but like her. Besides that, her temperament is perfect for golf."

Her coach at the university was Dale McNamara. She says, "A really good golfer has to be serious on the course. Nancy has that attitude. You can never tell how she is playing during a round, particularly if she is playing well. She also has tremendous powers of concentration. She can accomplish more in thirty minutes of practice than many people can in two hours. When she's on the course, she's pleasant, but she's all business."

"I just wasn't ready for how hard college is," says Nancy. "I had done well in high school. In fact, my parents wouldn't let me make a C. I also had a lot of restrictions when I was home. When I had a date, I had to be home by 10:30. Once I got to college, I had a hard time making myself study. I could stay out till two in the morning if I wanted. I just didn't know how to distribute my time."

After the National Collegiate Championship, Nancy quit school. At twenty she became a pro golfer. She joined the LPGA on July 29, 1977. That year, Nancy was named Rookie of the Year by *Golf Digest* magazine.

Nancy makes a chip shot.

When one man saw her play, he asked, "She's a rookie? When did she start playing, when she was two?"

Nancy has many golfer friends. "The Kid" is what other pros call her.

Judy Rankin, another LPGA member says, "They've got the wrong 'Wonder Woman' on TV."

Her followers call themselves "Nancy's Navy." Men and boys, women and girls, line up for her autograph. Nancy loves her fans. They shout for her to win. They cheer every shot—even during practice.

Tournament players do a lot of traveling. It's often fun and sometimes tiring. Traveling is part of the game, but sometimes players get homesick.

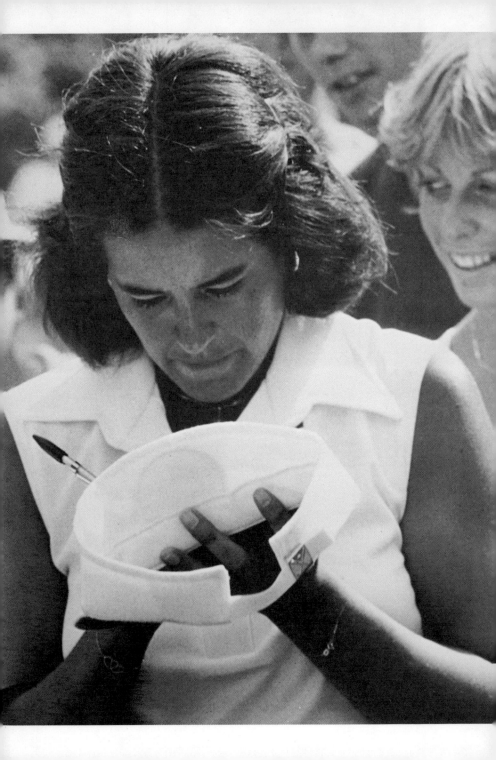

"One day at the Colgate European in London, I got a tremendous feeling of homesickness," Nancy says. "I had to get to a phone. It's funny, you don't realize how important your parents are until you leave."

Nancy's mother, Marina, died after an operation in September, 1977. Nancy dropped out of golfing for a month. She was sad. But, she became stronger.

Then she started golfing again. She won the tournament in Sarasota, Florida. She did it for her mother. "All I kept thinking about was her. After I won, I just cried and cried," said Nancy.

At age twenty-one, Nancy won the Colgate-Dinah Shore Winners Circle golf tournament in

Nancy and Roscoe wait to tee off. Nancy Whitworth, another LPGA player, waits too.

Palm Springs, California. As the LPGA rookie, she went on to win the Bent Tree Classic in Sarasota, Florida. Then she won the Sunstar Classic in Los Angeles. She missed her third straight victory in the Kathy Crosby/Honda Civic Classic. Sally Little won when Nancy was unable to sink her ball and lost by an inch.

"The best part of her game," her caddie Roscoe Jones says, ". . . must be her mental game. Yes. There she is, all sweet and smiling, kissing her daddy before the round. Then it's all business. She's got that ruthlessness. I can see her doing to the ladies what Nicklaus has done to the men."

Lining up a putt. Jane Blalock, another pro, says Nancy is "the best putter, male or female, in the game today."

JoAnne Carner says about Nancy, "She has all the shots, some which took me five years to develop. She certainly can play."

Nancy's answer to this is, "I just feel I'm going out there with nothing to lose."

But Nancy doesn't mention the hours she spends practicing. She has talent and ability to play. She also works to perfect her game. This is what makes Nancy Lopez a winner.

Some say, "Nancy Lopez is to golf what Chris Evert and Billie Jean King are to tennis."

Nancy smiles a lot. Her face lights up when she is standing over a ball. Then she becomes serious. She watches the ball with a steady eye. With a strong back swing, she brings the club down. She hits the ball with great power. Her swing looks awkward.

Lee Trevino watched Nancy play. He told her to use her swing as long as it works. "When it stops working, change," he said.

And when people bug her about her swing, she says, "Ever since Trevino told me to trust the swing I was born with, that's what I've done. You don't have to have some great swing to play golf. I've never had one and I've done well."

A friend of Nancy's and a great golfer herself, JoAnne Carner says about her, "She has confidence in her own ability. She's smart, because

Nancy hits the ball an average of 235 to 250 yards off the tee.

Nancy slams a fairway iron shot.

she doesn't listen to all the talk. She makes good changes, is a great trouble player . . ."

Her putting is said to be rare. "I have one weakness," Nancy admits. "That's my chipping. I guess I don't miss enough greens to get the practice."

Nancy has been called, "Long Ball" Lopez, for her long drives. Some think of her as Nancy Lopez "Windup Doll." They say, "All you have to do is turn the key and she hits the golf balls farther and straighter than almost any other woman."

Her caddie goes on to say, "She may be twenty-one, but there isn't another lady out there with more control."

There are many pressures in a game. Nancy must decide what shots are best.

Early in 1978 it looked as if Nancy had lost her control. She had zoomed to the top. Then something happened. It was at Mission Hills in California. She was up against a tough match. The first day out, Nancy shot four bogeys on the front nine. That was a lot of mistakes for Nancy. Things looked bad. Then on the last nine holes, she made three birdies. The next day Nancy made three bogeys the first seven holes. She made six birdies on the last ten.

This wouldn't be a bad score for most players, but Nancy was up against some good players. She was within four shots of winning. But that wasn't close enough. The next day was her worst round of the year. She trailed behind farther and farther. Finally Sandra Post beat her.

People and pressures can break anyone's game. Nancy had trouble during this tournament. Relatives and friends came to watch her play. Interviews with the press were heavy. To top it all off, her eight-year-old nephew ran around wearing a shirt that read, "AUNT NANCY NUMBER 1."

"People forgot that I'm human," Nancy said. "I don't feel happy right now."

Before her third tournament Nancy had said, "I have no pressures. It's just a game right now. When you're an amateur and you've won something already, you're expected to win every time out. Here we're nobodies."

Now Nancy's feeling the difference. She's into serious golf and she notices the change.

"My life is changing and I don't know if I want it to. So many things matter to me . . . how I look, how people feel about me, what my friends are doing. Now golf is so serious. The other day I told everybody, 'Look, this isn't a party. It's a golf tournament.' Then I felt terrible for being such a crab."

In May, 1978, Nancy won the Greater Baltimore Classic by three strokes.

"Great, super, fantastic, every good word I can think of," said Nancy after winning the LPGA in June 1978. After winning her fourth straight vic-

Nancy always wears her favorite gold cross in a tournament.

tory and becoming the earliest winner of $100,000 in a single season, she said. "And now that I've won four in a row, I'd like to break the record with five straight." And she did!

When Nancy was told that she played the last 41 holes without a bogey, she smiled and said, "Sounds good. I owe it to my putter."

In her rookie year (July 1977-July 1978) she won over $153,000. This was more than any rookie golfer, man or woman, had ever won.

Nancy played the Lady Keystone Open in June of 1978. She was interviewed before she played. Tom Melton interviewed her. Tom Melton is a sportscaster from Harrisburg, Pennsylvania.

Nancy drives the ball. Every shot is important to her.

Nancy liked Tom. Roscoe, Nancy's caddie, knew Nancy liked Tom. So Roscoe played cupid. He told Tom.

In August, Tom and Nancy said they would be married. They plan to marry April 14, 1979.

In 1978, Nancy won Rookie-of-the-Year and Player-of-the-Year honors. No pro golfer had won both honors before.

Nancy loves nice clothes and gold bracelets. She dresses in bright colors on and off the course.

Nancy says, "You think about people who work and play golf to relax. My work is playing golf. I can't do anything to relax. I can't swim because it's bad for my hands and grip. I can't play tennis because it builds up my arms. All I can do is dance and lie around in the sun." Then she adds with a smile, "But I do have my golf."

"My mother and father never pushed me to play golf. They let me follow my own course," Nancy says. "And I'm grateful to them for that."

Nancy Lopez, the pretty girl with dark hair and dark eyes, likes her career as a pro golfer. From the first day she heard the "cleats on the cement," she has pushed towards her goal. Her story is one of hard work. It has paid off for Nancy Lopez.

CHRONOLOGY

1963 — Started playing golf.

1966 — First tournament, won by 110 strokes

1969 — Won New Mexico Women's Amateur Title
— Won Western Amateur Championship

1970-75 — Won USGA Junior Girl's Title
— Won Women's NCAA
— Won Trans-national Championship
— Finished Third in U.S. Open
— Won thirteen AIAW Titles
— Won Bing Crosby National Pro-Am Title
— First girl to play on an all-male high school golf team. Helped win the State Championship in her junior year.

1976 — Won eight major amateur tournaments
— Won National Collegiate Championship

1977 — Dropped college and turned to playing pro golf
— Finished second in first three tournaments, including U.S. Open
— Won Kathryn Crosby Classic
— Won Los Angeles Sunstar Classic
— Named Rookie of the Year

1978 — Won 8 tournaments
— Became the earliest winner of $100,000 in a single season on an LPGA tour
— Became the all-time rookie money winner in pro golf, breaking Jerry Pate's 1976 earnings in the men's tour.
— Named LPGA Rookie of the Year
— Named LPGA Player of the Year

ABOUT THE AUTHOR

Nancy Robison had her first article published at the age of fifteen. It appeared in *The Christian Science Monitor* and was about her experiences as an actress on television. Since then, her career has bounced back and forth between writing and acting, modeling and dancing for movies and television. Now that her four sons are in college she has settled down to writing books for young people, playing tennis, skiing, and making guest appearances at schools and libraries. She has over fifteen books published and more on the way. Mrs. Robison lives in San Marino, California, with her husband and two of her four sons.